An Expert Guide to Stress Management

Dr Sarmila Sinha

Copyright © 2019 by Dr Sarmila Sinha

All rights reserved. No part of this book may be reproduced or transmitted in any form or by any means, including photocopying, recording or by any information storage and retrieval system for private and public use, without prior written permission of the author and/or publisher, except for the inclusion of brief quotations in articles and reviews. For permission requests or any query, write to the publisher, addressed 'Attention: Permissions Coordinator,' at the address below:

Living Life Stress Free Ltd.
P.O. Box 6945, London, W1A 6US, UK
info@livinglifestressfree.com
www.livinglifestressfree.com

Disclaimer

The purpose of this book is to educate and offer information of a general nature to help readers in their quest for stress management and general well-being. The author does not dispense medical advice or prescribe the use of any procedure, technique, medication or product as a form of treatment for physical, mental or medical problems without the help of a physician, either directly or indirectly. The author does not guarantee that anyone following the techniques, suggestions, tips, strategies, or advice will achieve success. The author/publisher shall have neither liability nor responsibility to anyone for any loss or damage caused, or alleged to be caused, by the information in this book.

Endorsement – Disclaimer

Reference made in this book to any product, company, process or service by trade name, generic name, trademark, and manufacturer or otherwise does not imply endorsement or sponsorship.

Preface

In the modern age, 'Stress' has become a household term, many identifying with it while trying to make sense of the fast-paced lifestyle and its impact on one's mental and physical health. While almost everyone can relate to stress and its effects, many don't realise how our day to day habits influence the extent to which stress affects us. And if we can make small changes in our lives, we can overcome stress or manage stress to a large extent.

This book gives the reader in-depth information about stress and its mechanism of action, the different triggers, its effects on the body and the mind. Most importantly the book gives the reader many strategies to overcome and manage stress. The book introduces a unique 4C approach to stress management (Calm, Clarity, Choice and Change), developed by Dr Sinha. She applies this unique 4C Approach to Stress Management in her workshops and courses for professionals and entrepreneurs. Attendees of the workshops have given highly positive feedback. One attendee wrote: *'Although it was practical, it had depth and I found myself connecting with very deep parts within me and even after the workshop I kept having important realisations about me and my life including past, present and future. It gave me much more than I had hoped for, and I feel the impact will go on beyond reducing stress. Some shifts took place right away, and some are still taking place now.'*

Acknowledgements

I want to dedicate this book to my late sister Joonaki, whose life was an inspiration to us all. She lived her life with incredible courage and kindness. Her transition from this world at an early age is a testimony to why we should all live our lives to the full and not hold back on our dreams. I also thank my family and friends for their love and support. I am immensely grateful to my teacher Swami Sivananda, for inspiring me with his unconditional love and compassion, which transcends the boundaries of race, religion and country.

TABLE OF CONTENTS

Chapter 1 An overview of Stress

Chapter 2 How Stress affects our body & mind

Chapter 3 What causes Stress in our lives?

Chapter 4 Managing Stress at Work

Chapter 5 Managing Stress in Difficult Communication

Chapter 6 Managing Stress in Relationships

Chapter 7 The 4C approach to stress management

Chapter 8 Making lifestyle changes

Chapter 9 Self-compassion, Self-love & positive affirmations

Chapter 10 Conclusion

References

Further reading

About the Author

Chapter 1 AN OVERVIEW OF STRESS

Stress is one of the most talked about topic; Google search engine statistics show that 'Stress' and 'Stress Management' is very commonly searched.

Did you know that the most commonly quoted treatment for stress is mindfulness and meditation - we all know this and yet how many of us practice meditation or deep breathing? Why do we struggle to translate knowledge into practice? I'm going to be brutally honest with you, and this will shake some of your beliefs. Are you ready to find out the answers?

I have been interested in this subject for several years. I have read many books, mostly motivational, and tried to seek answers on how to manage stress. My journey has been stressful at times – I failed to deal with stress despite my medical knowledge. That is when it hit me hard and challenged me as a doctor. Have I missed something here? Why can't I create results when the answers and methods are so bespoke and well laid out?

It was then I came to the realisation:

- there is a lot of difference between theory and practice
- there is a difference between how our analytical or human brain (frontal lobe and parietal lobes) and our instinctive brain (the primitive brain or limbic system) acts. Sometimes when we face stress, it is our primitive brain that takes over - so-called fight or flight response- I'll describe this later.
- human beings are creatures of habit. We are stuck in our pattern of thoughts and actions, sometimes we are on autopilot, and we repeat our unhelpful behaviours out of habit more than anything else.

- what drives us into action is mostly either Fear or Joy.
- fear leads to stressful work or response while joy leads to inspired action.
- we have a hidden power that we can tap into to overcome this habit of thought or action.

I want to share with you a powerful exercise below. It will help you question the negative thoughts that are usually the mental blocks to achieving success and can lead to stress and worry.

Exercise

Where do you see yourself when you say these words to yourself?

I hope	Is there despair?
I wish	Deprived?

I want	Lacking?

In a state of 'wanting', rather than focusing your thoughts and energy towards your goals and to the positive things you have, you are focused on the negative aspects of your life. Negative thoughts, ruminations, and lack of self-confidence originate from negative thought processes that do not amplify your potentials or capabilities.

Stress can originate from a place of 'want' or 'lack,' and fear can be one of the main reasons for stress.

Exercise

What are your fears – I have listed some examples, and you could add more to the list:

Fear of failure or not excelling (in a job, exam, projects, etc.)

Fear of commitment (in a relationship)
Fear of being abandoned (relationship break-up etc.)
Fear of letting down your team, poor performance for athletes
Fear of facing criticism, making mistakes at work, of being judged unfavourably
Concern as a parent (of not able to deal with your child's issues)
Fear of losing money, failing health
Fear of the unknown

When you are experiencing Fear, it triggers the stress response, and if this happens regularly, then it can give rise to chronic stress.

Remember:

- our problems are only as big as we think or believe them to be; in most cases, we tend to magnify our questions and worries.
- learning to think and look at a problem in its right perspective requires skill and practice. You will begin to believe that you are not part of the problem, but you belong to part of the solution.

So, what is the definition of stress?

Stress is the overall physiological and psychological impact on a person in response to adverse or uncomfortable actual events or perceived events.

Stress can occur acutely in response to specific triggers and can resolve when the trigger is absent. On the other hand, stress can persist and be an ongoing occurrence in response to repeated triggers or perceived triggers. These triggers are also known as stressors.

Stress is also known as tension, mental pressure or strain, and worry. It is described by some as a state of intense anxiety and worry.

Hans Selye, a Hungarian endocrinologist, was one of the early researchers of stress. He observed in medical school that people who had chronic illnesses like TB and cancer appeared to have some common factors which we now call 'stress'.
He coined the term 'general adaptation syndrome' or 'Selye's syndrome' which includes three different responses of the body on exposure to stressful events such as cold, surgery, or chemicals. These three responses are initial alarm followed by a stage of resistance or adaptation and finally, a phase of exhaustion and ultimately death. Selye also first described how the body copes with stress with the help of the Hypothalamic-pituitary-adrenal axis (HPA) axis. The fight or flight reaction is part of the 'general adaptation syndrome,' as defined by Hans Selye in 1936.

Selye also classified stress into two main types-good stress known as 'Eustress' and bad stress known as 'Distress.' He mentioned that in both states, there is stress response leading to an increase of cortisol. Eustress state often leads to increased productivity, is invigorating and linked with a positive goal setting.

Acute Stress Reaction (also known as a mental shock) is a psychiatric diagnosis characterized by a critical psychological reaction in response to traumatic events. It is not the same as the term "stress" which we use in our day to day lives. Distress, on the other hand, leads to increased anxiety, worry without an outlet for positive action.

Prevalence of Stress in the UK:

A recent survey found that over the past year, almost three quarters (74%) of people have at some point felt so stressed that they felt overwhelmed or unable to cope. The survey, commissioned by the

Mental Health Foundation and undertaken by YouGov, polled 4,169 adults in the UK in 2018. This stress study had a sample size of 4,619 respondents. Another recent poll concurs with this finding with 82% of people feeling stressed at least sometime during a typical week, and eight per cent that felt stressed all the time.

One area that is frequently researched is stress at work. Around half a million people are experiencing work-related stress in the UK.

Chapter 2 How Stress Affects Our Body & Mind

A stress reaction is a normal healthy response to any threat, as it prepares the body to respond to the risk as a part of the body's defence mechanism. It plays a crucial role in survival. It was highly relevant thousands of years ago when we had to defend ourselves from actual threats such as wild animals in the forests. But in the modern era, we live quite safe and secure lives, and we are not exposed to life or death situations regularly. Unfortunately, our body does not distinguish between the different sources of stress, e.g., a sabre-toothed tiger or meeting a deadline at work would have a similar stress response.

The other problem is that in the modern age, we face more frequent stressful situations. Therefore, for some people, the body is continuously on high alert or in a constant state of stress. This has health implications, and we will discuss this later in this chapter.

Stress manifests through two main pathways:

A.   Adrenaline or Epinephrine

B.   Cortisol

A) The nervous system, in particular, the autonomic nervous system (ANS), in the body, regulates the body's response to stressful events. The brain communicates by releasing chemicals known as neurochemicals. The word 'neuro' means 'relating to nerve cells, or neurons'. Neurons are cells that are present in the brain and the nervous system. Neurons communicate with each other through chemical messengers known as neurotransmitters.

The autonomic nervous system releases adrenaline or epinephrine – this gives rise to a set of responses which are collectively known as 'fight or flight' reaction.

Physiological effect: these include the symptoms manifested by the body through the release of adrenaline and noradrenaline:

- increased or raised heart rate
- fast breathing or increased frequency of respiration
- tightening of the muscles
- rise in blood pressure
- increased blood flow to skeletal muscles
- glucose released by the liver
- increased blood flow to the heart and the brain
- sweating
- increased activity of the digestive system and bladder system.

B) Cortisol is also referred to as the stress hormone. It is produced by the pyramid-shaped adrenal glands, which are located just above the kidneys. The adrenal gland gets the signal to release cortisol from the pituitary gland (located in the brain). Cortisol helps in the fight or flight reaction by helping the body respond to danger in the following ways:

- increases the blood sugar level thus providing the body with the energy to act
- breaks down protein and mobilizes fat
- regulates blood pressure
- reduces allergic and inflammatory responses of the body.

While the above symptoms are all seen in Acute Stress (not synonymous with Acute Stress Reaction), prolonged exposure to stress leads to chronic stress.

Continued high levels of cortisol in the body has some adverse effects such as low immunity, thus making the body prone to infections, weight gain, high blood pressure and a host of other health consequences. Below is a list of some long-term effects of chronic stress:

Effect on Cardiovascular health and Metabolic system	High blood pressure, raised Cholesterol, increased weight and obesity, coronary artery disease, diabetes.
Effect on the Immune System	Reduced immunity leading to frequent colds, chest infection.
Effect on Cognition	Poor concentration, inability to retain new information leading to memory problems.
Effect on Circadian	Insomnia – inability to fall

Rhythm	asleep, disturbed sleep.
Impact on Mental state	Irritability, anxiety, anger, low mood, feeling helpless or hopeless, panic attacks, racing thoughts, poor self-esteem, poor motivation., depression, and personality changes.
Effect on Hormone levels	Increased prolactin levels leading to fertility problems, raised cortisol levels, thyroid hormone abnormalities
Effect on Behaviour	Compensatory self- help behaviours such as drinking excess alcohol, smoking, excess caffeine, or any other illicit substances. Some people use gambling as an escape from

	stress.

Exercise:

Reflect on how frequent your experience of day to day stressors are – examples of ongoing stress could be financial difficulties, a challenging conversation and so on. I would not advice to recollect traumatic memories as this is not the scope of this exercise. **If you are experiencing very low mood, flashbacks and intense emotions, my advice is to not to do this exercise but seek professional help via your GP, physician or a registered counsellor.** If you are unsure about your symptoms, you may benefit from reading this book: 'Depression A Guide to Recovery'.

For the purpose of this exercise, choose a low-grade stressful event from your life:

- identify the trigger, what set it off
- what were the symptoms experienced, and how long did it last?
- how did you react to the stress – was it a fight response or a flight response?

Stress Journal: Having a stress journal can be a helpful tool to jot down different triggers for stress in your lives as they could vary from person to person. You could keep a log of such events for 2-4-week time period – this is a good way to analyse the difficult areas in your life.

In the next chapter I will go through the different causes or predisposing factors of stress. You may want to take notes how these factors are relevant in your case.

Chapter 3 WHAT CAUSES STRESS IN OUR LIVES?

Stress can be broadly classified into the above types.

1. Physical stress or External stress
2. Psychological Stress or Internal stress
3. Chemical Stress

I have listed examples of each type of stress under the broad headings in tabulated form.

1) Physical stress	Accidents, trauma, poor light, loud noise, etc.
2) Psychological Stress	Difficult relationship, poor communication, bullying, employment and financial difficulties etc.

3) Chemical Stress	Hormones, heavy metal, infections (bacteria, viruses, fungi)

Not everyone reacts to Stress in the same way. Our past experiences influence how we react to adverse circumstances. I have listed the common factors that influence how we react to Stress.

a) Personality types
b) Genetic factors
c) Environmental and Social Stressors
d) Life events including Childhood experiences (major traumas).

a) Personality Types:

Myers Briggs developed the 16 personality types, which can be a useful tool in predicting the behaviours and attitudes of people. This was inspired by the original work of Carl Jung on Personality types. Myers Briggs proposed the 16-personality types, which later became the MBTI structured assessment tool to assess personality types. The 16 personality types are typically described in abbreviated form of four letters: e.g., INFP: Introversion (I), Intuition (N), Feeling (F), Perception (P).

Another model is the Five-factor model, which is widely used to describe personality types. It was developed by Robert McCrae and Paul Costa. Psychologist Lewis Goldberg further described each of these five personality types using an inventory known as the International Personality Item Pool (IPIP). Some of the characteristics of these five personality types are as follows:

1. Openness to experience: People in this category are open to new ideas, curious, and creative. People

in this category are assessed along a continuum, with 'inventive' and 'curious' at one end and 'being consistent and cautious' at the other. A high degree of openness is associated with being very creative and thrill-seeking, while a low degree of transparency is associated with minimal risk-taking.

2. Conscientiousness: People in this category are self-disciplined and organized. They plan ahead rather than act spontaneously. Sometimes people with great honesty can be misinterpreted as being stubborn and obsessed.

3. Extraversion: People are marked on a continuum that goes from being outgoing and energetic to being solitary and reserved. Highly extroverted people are often thought of as oppressive, while introverted people are relatively reserved in social situations.

4. Agreeableness: People of this personality type are friendly and compassionate when they are highly agreeable, whereas low-agreeable personalities are often challenging, detached, or competitive.

5. Neuroticism: This is the most essential personality type when discussing causative factors for stress and depression. This personality type is associated with being sensitive and nervous at one extreme, to being secure and confident at the other. Highly neurotic individuals are vulnerable to negative emotions like anger, anxiety, and depression, and generally, have poor psychological well-being.

b) Genetic factors:

There is a close link between depression and stress. People who go on to develop depression and other mood disorders have pre-existing stressful life events. But not everyone who is exposed to stress become depressed – there is a role of genetic factors in determining vulnerability to developing depression and other mental illnesses in response to high levels of stress. There is an epigenetic mechanism to link early life adversity and sensitivity to stressful life events in adulthood. The following genes - 5HTTLPR, BDNF have been linked with depression and bipolar in response to highly stressful events.

David Goldman found gene variants that affected the response or expression of Neuropeptide Y (NPY). NPY is located in the brain and other tissues, it is produced in response to stress, and it reduces anxiety. NPY also regulates appetite, weight, and emotional response. Genetic variants of NPY account for maladaptive stress response, and this often underlies mental disorders such as depression. Low levels of NPY leads to reduced stress tolerance and a heightened sense of anxiety.

c) Environmental and Social stressors:

Environmental stressors are factors that are present in the environment that could affect the human body adversely in the form of stress. They could also have long term health implications, such as developing chronic physical and mental health conditions.

Exposure to natural disasters and electromagnetic radiation are rare and extreme forms of environmental stressors, but there may be more common and less severe forms of stressors such as poor lighting, loud noise, and poor posture.

Any microorganisms such as viruses, bacteria, fungi as well as allergens also form part of environmental stressors.

Work-related stressors include – Health and safety breaches at the workplace, heavy labour, noise pollution, etc.

Social stressors include the following:

- reduced social interaction or social isolation
- bullying, racism and other forms of social discrimination
- poor communication or difficult communication
- difficult relationships.

d) Life events, including adverse childhood experiences:

Any significant life events could be a cause of stress. Again, not everyone is predisposed to stress at every life event. I have listed some life events that could lead to stress:

- any trauma to the body- accidents, surgery.
- childhood trauma such as parental loss, neglect, bullying, and any form of abuse.
- separation or divorce
- loss of job or job role

- financial loss
- change of job, relocation
- changes in life routine, such as being a new parent, marriage, etc.

Exercise:

In our courses and workshops, we go through the wheel of life identifying areas that are less fulfilling and identifying areas that can be improved. We have the wheel of life template to score: 1, being the lowest score and 10 being the best score. Once you identify areas of your life that are possible triggers of stress you can then actively seek to improve these areas.

Personalized Stress Assessment: The following is a personalised stress assessment that we do in our courses - This assessment, can be personalized and tailored to each individual, it can be done by the stress management coach at one of the sessions or can be done by the client. Time needed to complete is approx. 30 minutes. I have scored them as follows:

1 = Never or Not Applicable

2 = Rarely (once every few weeks)

3 = Less Frequently (once every 1-2 weeks)

4 = Commonly (at least once a week)

5 = More Frequently (few days a week or once a day)

6 = Always (Daily or few times a day)

Questions	1	2	3	4	5	6
I take at least 3 meals a day						
I eat until I feel very full						
I eat when I feel hungry						
I have fixed sleep routine (e.g., 10PM till 6 AM)						
I can fall asleep within minutes of lying						

in bed						
I use Tech/phones/TV etc. in my bed before going to bed						
I have a disturbed sleep pattern						
I wake up early morning feeling fatigued and tired						
I have trouble focusing or concentrating						
I feel irritable, angry, and often regret my anger outbursts						
I feel anxious before an important meeting, deadline, or presentation						
I struggle to communicate with my boss, peers at work						
I'm struggling in my relationship with my family/spouse or friends						
I consume more than the recommended alcohol limit per week						
I smoke excess of 10 cigarettes a day						
I take other drugs/out of counter pills						

to calm myself						
I have chronic physical health condition/s						
I am struggling to achieve my goals						

Once the questionnaire is completed, the client and the coach discuss the areas that needs to be improved upon. A follow-up assessment is done after the allocated time- a minimum of 12-16 weeks.

Chapter 4 MANAGING STRESS AT WORK

The World Health Organisation (WHO) has defined 'burnout' as a specific state of psychological stress caused by an individual's workplace and/or occupation. The symptoms of burnout are emotional exhaustion, depersonalisation, and reduced feelings of personal accomplishment.

Stress at work may not be evident because of one or more the following reasons:

- first job, wanting to impress seniors
- everyone seems to be working hard, so you don't want to be the one complaining
- feeling under pressure to meet deadlines
- reluctant to seek help as it may go against you when it comes to getting a bonus or raise

- personal difficulties that you are keen to keep private, but you are struggling to have a work-life balance
- working long shifts, which is impacting your sleep, you are hesitant to approach your boss for a change in working hours as nobody seems to complain
- struggling to keep up with work demands and always feels like 'catching up' and never really 'on top of everything'
- no breaks at work, often eating your lunch at the work desk
- struggling to socialize at work, no one seems interested, and it feels like they are avoiding
- poor self-esteem and confidence, feeling out of depth.

Alternately you may be the boss or a senior manager at your work and experiencing stress due to one of these reasons (this list is not exhaustive):

- newly appointed boss, do not know the team well and are struggling to find your feet
- was part of the group, and suddenly you are the boss, which you perceive is affecting your relationship with your peers
- pressure from senior management or corporate to meet specific targets, and you have to delegate tasks now - you were never a bossy person, so you are worried how this suddenly affects your image. You dread other people calling you 'bossy' etc.
- you have to fire people at work, have difficult conversations with your employees, and you are struggling to fit into this new role.

There may be a host of other reasons for experiencing stress at work. Sometimes people simply deny that they are stressed as they feel it's a reflection of their weakness - which is not true!

In 2008, Dame Carol Black in her comprehensive review of the health of UK's working-age population concluded that ill health of staff contributes adversely to the economy of the country so much so that its cost is similar in magnitude to paying for a second National Health Service (NHS) (Black, 2008).

The NICE (National Institute of Clinical Excellence) guidelines titled 'Workplace Health: management practices' were published in 2015 and updated in 2016, which laid emphasis on positive leadership traits among managers such as being open and approachable and encouraging new ideas, which can improve the health and well-being of staff. NICE also recommends that health and well-being policies are included in the induction, training, and development of a new team.

In October 2017, an independent review titled 'Thriving at Work' led by Stevenson and Farmer was published by the UK government. It stated that every year, 300,000 people lose their jobs due to mental health problems, and the review looked at how employers can support their employees to thrive at work even when experiencing mental health problems. The report also recommended that the three largest public sector employers – the National Health Service (NHS), Education and Civil service put emphasis on areas with a higher risk of stress and to support mental health issues of its employees.

Reducing Stress at Work:

Stress can affect the productivity of the staff and the employer overall. Common factors that can lead to stress at work include workload or capacity issues, staff burnout, not having protected break-time, etc.

I would like to share some useful tips which, being a health and well-being ambassador, I used to plan and facilitate along with the other ambassadors at my NHS workplace. Each month, a healthy tip of the month was circulated across the Trust or organisation. Mindfulness groups were arranged in different parts so that staff could use the space to relax and reflect. Based on feedback from staff, a range of initiatives was put in place by the ambassadors. One example is the development of activity corners in team bases, which were equipped with puzzles, games, and activities for staff to use during their break time.

You could start your own health and wellbeing group at your workplace and take initiatives to help yourself and your colleagues.

#Exercise

Reflect on your work schedule and work life and make a list of things that are working very well for you. Next, make a list of goals or upcoming targets that you have to meet.

Make a list of your positive attributes and how you are going to amplify your strengths to achieve your goal.

Is there any area at your work which you would like to improve?

The following strategies can be applied at work to manage or reduce work stress:

1. Knowing your potential as well as limitation: Sometimes we take on more work than feasible which leads to stress. This can be due to lack of awareness of the task involved, lacking assertiveness to say 'no' to a task assigned and so on. In our courses, we emphasise on assertive training, setting healthy boundaries between us

and our colleagues and also how to seek help in difficult situations.

2. Having regular supervision and self-reflection: This is very helpful especially if you are new in the job or a trainee. Don't skip or postpone supervision as they may be valuable in providing you guidance on how to navigate your way in the job. Some organisations provide mentorship, and this can be done by a senior colleague, not necessarily a manager or your boss. Note down your challenges at your workplace, for doctors- you can discuss difficult cases and so on.

3. Having a peer group – In the medical profession, there are peer groups where the doctors meet regularly with their group to discuss career plans, self-development plans and any courses of interest. This model can easily be replicated to other professions as well. You may already meet up with your work

colleagues over drinks at the pub on a Friday evening – you can have informal meetings to discuss your work challenges and brainstorm ideas on how to improve the work load etc.

4. Having regular breaks at work: This is very important for people who have desk jobs and sit for long hours in front of the computer screens. Screen fatigue, poor posture, poor light etc. are common causes of work-related stress. You may want to have regular breaks where you make it a point to walk to the coffee machine or walk to discuss an assignment with your colleague rather than doing this over the phone. Waking improves the blood flow in the body and it gives the eyes the much-needed break. In the summer, consider eating lunch in your office grounds. These are some ideas, but you can come up with more creative ideas on how to have relaxing breaks. Don't use your breaks to call or check your mobile phones or social

media as that would not be considered as a relaxing break. Taking time out to be with family and friends and taking regular breaks from work is essential to reduce stress. When you are working full-time or long hours, you give work a lot of your time and energy. When you are working against pressures such as meeting deadlines, achieving targets or managing teams, the added responsibility can be a cause of long-term stress and burnout. However, you can address this by having an honest and open discussion with your boss. It is essential to recognise early signs of stress–such as fatigue, eye strain, irritability, headaches, not sleeping well–so that you can take steps to reduce your stress. I have listed some ideas you can use to reduce stress at work: • Taking regular breaks: No matter how busy you are, ensure you take frequent breaks by moving away from your desk, going for a walk at lunchtime, or doing some stretches in your office if possible.

5. Resolving any conflict: This can be done by speaking to your manager. It is essential to get as much support as possible. If you do not say you are having problems, other staff might not notice. It is better to raise concerns at an early stage. • Workload: If you like to please others and struggle to say 'no,' you may find yourself taking on a more significant workload than you can manage. It is essential to know your limitations and take care not to overstretch yourself. There are many other stress-relieving strategies, such as going part-time or working flexible hours, if you can afford it. Being honest and upfront, if you are experiencing stress and burnout, is better than trying even harder at work, hoping the stress will go away by itself. Doing chair yoga, stretching and deep breathing exercises can be done for up to 5 minutes.

Again, this is something we teach in our courses.

6. Practising Compassion and Gratitude at work place improves our relationship with our peers and seniors. It also improves our confidence and removes the blame culture.
7. Mindfulness can also be applied at work place. Mindfulness training is available through trained psychologist. It is easy to learn and practice mindfulness – as it improves our awareness of our environment and allows us to observe and accept the reality as it is rather than use our judgement or preconceptions to interpret situations. Mindfulness is a powerful tool, if you can apply at your work place. It allows one to focus on the present moment, on the 'here and now'. Research has proved that mindfulness is an effective strategy or tool for stress management, and you can easily apply this at work.

8. Meditation is also another useful tool to counteract stress at work. Most people relate meditation with religion or saints but actually anyone can meditate. The simplest definition of meditation I have come across is letting the mind go, not to dwell on any thoughts. It is almost impossible for the mind to be still, it will jump from one topic to another. Most people get hooked on to the thoughts and allow the emotions associated with the thought overcome them. In meditation, it is advised to let the mind wander and observe the thoughts from a distance and not own or associate with any of the thoughts. Focussing on one's own breathing helps in meditation.
9. Time Management: When you have a big project or assignment, it is natural to feel stressed and feel the adrenaline pumping. While this may be helpful in the initial stages as it will get you up and running, having the stress for

prolonged periods of time is actually counterproductive and it reduces productivity. This is explained with the following diagram:

Stress Curve

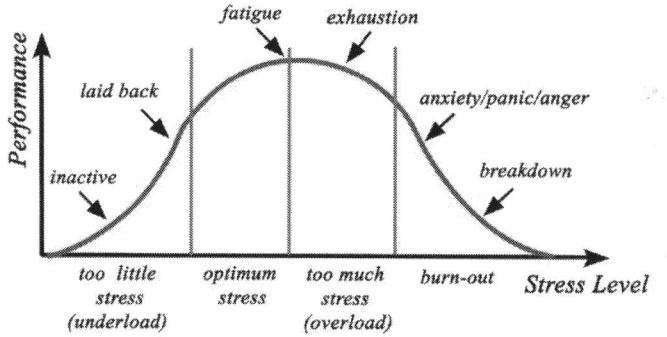

So, the best way to proceed in this scenario is to break the task into bite-size smaller assignment – you may even want to delegate some aspect of the work to your juniors in exchange of a 'mention' in the project and so on. You can be further creative in planning the task way ahead of completion date and have small celebrations as you steadily progress. So, the key is getting big projects completed is: PREPARE, PLAN, DELEGATE.

10. Keeping well hydrated and having healthy snacks at work reduces fatigue and keeps the brain active. Dehydration can lead to many health issues such as headache, poor concentration, constipation and so on.

11. Having Health and Wellbeing Champions at workplace is a good and effective way to discuss Stress at work and initiate projects or steps to reduce work stress. In 2018, I was a Health and Wellbeing ambassador for doctors in the NHS, there were a total of 75 ambassadors in the NHS Trust. Our role was to support our colleagues locally by **arranging meetings, listening to any concerns and supporting in resolving any issues. We actively promoted Healthy lifestyle by raising awareness of healthy eating, exercise, organising "Walking" events and giving out**

incentives such as discount on gym memberships. Celebrating the good work of the staff also was an important part of our role.

All employers have a responsibility to ensure health and wellbeing of its employees. It helps in improving the productivity of the organisation, boosts the morale of its staff as they feel well supported.

Chapter 5 MANAGING STRESS IN DIFFICULT COMMUNICATION

Communication in difficult situations or circumstances can be challenging and can be a cause of significant stress.

Communication is of mainly two types – verbal and non-verbal. Non-verbal can be of several ways such as written, sign language and digital. Digital communication can be via email, text, social media such as Twitter, Instagram, Facebook, etc.

In the modern age, people rely more on the digital form of communication rather than face to face. This is a type of indirect contact where two people do not have to meet in person, and communication is via the digital platform.

In face to face contact, non-verbal communication can be through body language such as eye contact, stance or posture, and other gestures.

In verbal communication, the tone and rate of speech are also important rather than just the content. For example, if someone is shouting or yelling out loud while communicating, it often implies that the person is angry, excited or distressed.

Examples of poor communication are:

- Poor body language:
    1. Hands clenched or arms folded
    2. Loud tone or pitch
    3. Invading personal space of others.

    Ideally, you should be at the same level as the other person while speaking.

- Relying entirely on emails or other non-verbal means of communication rather than face to face if both are working at the same office or department. Sometimes it is better to meet up in person or at least discuss over the phone. Emails and letters are considered more formal means of communication.

- Minimal eye contact while communicating: At home, sometimes we are busy looking at our computer screens or other devices while our partner or child is talking to us. This conveys a message that either you are not interested in the conversation or you are not paying attention. The other person often will feel unappreciated or unheard. This is applicable among friends in a social circle or at work too.

- Avoidance: Sometimes, we put off an awkward conversation by postponing or finding excuses not to discuss the issues – these are examples of poor or ineffective communication as matters can get worse or not resolved by this method.

Exercise:

Can you find other examples of poor communication and how would you like to resolve awkward conversation?

Strategies for effective communication: In chapter 7, I have described the 4C (Calm, Clarity, Choice and Change) approach to Stress Management – these strategies can be applied when you are anticipating a difficult conversation or communication. But I have specified some important and specific strategies that can be applied in the field of effective communication.

1. Plan your meeting: This is often underestimated but planning a meeting helps in organising your thoughts and getting your agenda in order. There is no harm in mentally rehearsing the conversation or at least the opening

statement. When meeting for an important business deal, you want to come across as confident and highly efficient. Sometimes, first impressions matter – your first meeting could make or break a deal. Rather than spending time worrying, you can take steps to prepare yourself for the important meeting. The same is applicable for job interviews. My advice is to always start a meeting with a friendly gesture – offer of handshake and a smile. If you are hosting the meeting do not forget to offer a drink. This could simply be a glass of water. If you are hosting the meeting at your office, pay attention to the environment – the temperature of the room, any rubbish and a cluttered desk. If you are doing a presentation, make sure you have checked your presentation, always take a charger with you for your laptop or notepad. If you are preparing for an interview, make sure your CV is up to date, take print outs of your CV to share with the panel.

2. Dressing appropriately: Pay attention to the dress code when meeting clients or at job interviews. Have a spare set of formal wear that is fresh from the dry cleaners and ensure your shoes are sparkling clean. As I said, first impressions matter and could be your only chance to impress. Preparing for job interviews or an important business deal can be very stressful, but you can minimise stress by planning well ahead of the meeting. I have done a checklist below which you can use in all important meetings.

3. Table: Checklist for important appointments/presentations/meetings:

Phase 1. Planning:	- Send diary invites to the relevant people, specify the date, time and

(3-4 months prior)	venue of the meeting. Earn appreciation by sending map or directions and any parking facilities, asking for dietary preferences if you are planning to provide meals. - Book the venue well in advance or request your secretary to book this for you. - Always give your clients/attendees the option to contact you for any queries, - You can email the agenda well in advance. Nobody likes guesswork and you will be thanked for the time and effort you have put in getting this together. - Planning well in advance also gives you lot of time to prepare each and every topic on the agenda. - Book any speakers/services well in advance if needed.

	- If you are travelling out of town for the meeting, make sure that you start booking the tickets, hotel rooms etc. If you are travelling abroad, don't forget to check your passport expiry date whether you need to reapply for passport/visa etc. - If you need to apply for annual leave or arrange cover at work, now is the time to start planning.
Phase 2. Planning and Preparation: (4- 6 weeks prior)	- Start preparing the presentation if you are expected to present at the meeting, - Start researching for any updates on your topic, the latest information and run through the questions you might be asked. - If you are submitting or presenting a project, it must be finished by this stage and you should be at the final draft stage. If you have too many unfinished projects, it's best

to focus on the ones that you have finished already and are confident to deliver well.
- Go through your wardrobe – Buy any essentials, wear the dress again, see if you are comfortable wearing it.
- You may start contacting your clients and attendees to check if they wanted anything added to the agenda. This is an indirect way of getting them interested in the meeting and also confirming their attendance. Offer any assistance or try to help them resolve any queries. If your attendees are travelling from out of town, they will appreciate your help in booking hotels/cabs/airport pick up and so on.
- On the other hand, if you are travelling, book airport pick-up, arrange foreign currency and buy appropriate clothing depending on

	the weather of your destination. - If you have pets, arrange for pet home, speak with your family and friends and arrange for any house maintenance in your absence. - Check your diary if you need to rearrange any appointments (e.g., dental appointment) which coincides at the time of your visit.
Phase 3. Final preparation: 3-4 days prior.	- If it is an important meeting where you are expected to do a presentation, it must be ready by now and go through it few times. - Your ticket and foreign currency (if applicable) must be with you by now. - If you are on prescription pills, make sure you have enough to take for the journey – see your GP or doctor to get repeat prescription if needed. - Always ensure that you have a

	first aid box, phone and laptop chargers in your suitcase if you are travelling. - The next few days focus on eating and sleeping well, avoid late night parties if possible.
Phase 4: Delivery phase:	- This is the phase where you must now deliver. The focus is arriving on time, maintaining calm, feeling confident. Keep well hydrated, take deep breaths be positive. Don't let any negative thoughts dominate your mind, keep clear headed. If you are doing a presentation, meeting business clients or doing a job interview, then you are in focus and the pressure of being judged or interviewed can be very stressful. However as long as you have planned and prepared well, you can relax during the actual

	meeting.

4. This scenario is for situations where you have to meet someone to discuss a conflict at work or in personal life circumstance. Try to meet up and discuss issues face to face: Be open-minded and listen. Being a good listener is one of the key attributes of a great communicator. Sometimes a good ear is all that takes to resolve a conflict or misunderstanding. This can be applied both at work and at home. When listening, it is better to give full attention too – making eye contact, facing them and not being distracted by your phone or computer when they are speaking.

5. Look for things in common: if you can start off a conversation with a note of appreciation for the other person, this can act as an ice breaker. Everyone has positive

attributes or qualities, for e.g., one may be a good timekeeper or a good accountant. If you can capitalise on the strengths of the other person, they will reciprocate with a positive or at least a neutral tone. I am not telling you to sing false praises as that will be spotted. Also don't hesitate to appreciate the other person.

6. Don't rush to a conclusion or take sides (this is applicable if you are the boss and you have to resolve conflict). Don't send off that angry email!

7. Seek help from seniors if needed. If you are in an entry position or a trainee, it is very important to keep the lines of communication open with your seniors and peers. There will be many opportunities to learn new skills.

8. Seeking conflict resolution via managers or seniors if the initial stage of communication

does not resolve conflict. This is relevant for mediation at workplace when there is more than one area of conflict or if it is an ongoing issue. It may be helpful to write down the different issues.

9. Be honest and admit limitations – this lets down the guard, and people appreciate honesty in general.

In our courses and workshop, we given scenarios where the attendees have to practise different challenging scenarios and we focus on the communication style. Assertive communication is needed in certain areas and we teach practical ways to improve assertive communication which also improves the confidence level.

From experience, I can say that that the qualities that stand the test of time and yield benefit in the long run are:

- Being open and honest
- Planning the response and avoiding hasty decisions
- Practising 'Calm' before an important meeting through deep breathing, meditation and other tools
- Keeping the lines of communication open

Poor communication or ineffective communication can have an impact on our relationships at work as well as home. I have described this further in the next chapter.

Chapter 6 MANAGING STRESS IN RELATIONSHIPS

It is no understatement that we all lead busy lives, juggling work, caring for our children, household chores and other activities. It is worth mentioning that the things that grab our attention are the 'problems' in our lives. We take for granted the things that are working well for us. This is particularly true in case of our relationships. Being distracted by our problems, we often prioritise these issues. Every relationship is built on the foundation of mutual love, respect, trust and commitment. No matter how busy you are, it is very important to give some time from your busy day to nourish and nurture your relationships. We all wear multiple hats when it comes to relationships, we are most of these to different people in our lives – we are a partner, spouse, parent, child, friend, peer, boss, manager, uncle or aunt, grandparent and so on. You need to decide how much time you will give to maintain a loving and caring relationship. It is important to be open and honest with our loved ones. If you are going through a tough time, it is better to at least share that you are going to be busy for the next few months and may not be available for other commitments. We sometimes try to protect our loved ones by not sharing our problems with them – for example, in case of financial difficulties. It is a balance of how much information you want to share – your loved ones, as they will know that something is not right, even though you don't share anything.

The psychological impact of stress such as low mood, irritability, poor sleep, inability to take pleasure in activities and so on also affect our relationships. It's a double whammy because our other stressors will lead to relationship stress.

That's why it's very important to communicate with our loved ones.

I have listed some common causes of stress in family relationships, and as I mentioned earlier, poor communication can contribute or worsen the different types of relationship stressors and how to manage them:

Trust issues, lack of commitment: Checking in with your partner and spouse every now and then boosts the healthy trusting relationship. Celebrate your anniversaries with much enthusiasm, give each other gifts on special occasion. Book a dinner date every now and then when you both are busy and spend less quality time with each other because of your busy schedule. If it very difficult, if not impossible to repair a broken trust. Infidelity is the number one cause of Mistrust in a relationship, many marriages ended in divorce because of this. Hence if you are serious about your relationship, come clean and honest if you have fallen off the wagon. But if this becomes a pattern, then the relationship will surely suffer.

Different priorities, feeling ignored or let down: If you are in a long-term relationship with your partner, sometimes priorities change. An open and honest conversation will save you and your partner from any unnecessary stress about the future of your relationship. Don't assume that your partner will understand everything or will automatically support you every time. For example, you may want to have an adventure holiday, but your partner may simply want to relax at home. Many families have dinner table discussions about their upcoming plans or wishes – this is a good way of communicating your wishes and checking with what the rest of the family wants. If you are the parent, you have an added responsibility to ensure that the children are well entertained during their holidays and sharing the parental role between you and your partner needs good teamwork. Checking each other's availability, booking leave from work, booking holidays well in advance saves one from stress. People feel ignored if their wishes are ignored time and again – this is true also in the case of children and teenagers. When you have a teenager, they want their voices to be heard, they want to be treated as equal, with respect and so on. So, no matter who you are speaking with or dealing with, pay full attention when you are having a conversation. On the other hand, if you feel that someone is ignoring you as they are facing the computer while you speak or texting someone else or doing other chores, do not hesitate to politely point this behaviour out to them as they may be completely unaware that their behaviour is letting you down. This scenario can happen with parents too when dealing with their children. You can point this out by saying in a polite way – *'I can see that you are busy on your (phone/computer etc.) This is an important topic and I want your undivided attention while I speak. I'm happy to wait for a few minutes while you finish your task at hand or give me a suitable time when I can discuss this again'*. Remember most relationship problems happen because of misunderstandings and in most cases the other person is not aware that they are hurting your feelings. So before assuming the worst, it is important to speak your thoughts aloud in a non-confrontational and non-judgemental way, keeping the lines of communication open.

As parents, the challenge becomes apparent when your little angel starts pre-teen years and onto becoming a teenager. Suddenly you are no longer the centre of attachment, the go to person. They suddenly seem to know more than you, even lecture you on certain topics and their favourite word is *'No or nope'*. They develop habits that scare you such as spending hours and hours on the internet, chatting, gaming and so on. Your worst fears suddenly grip you and you feel helpless in this situation. My advice is to plan your parenting early on, teach discipline early on, have house rules and be true to them yourself. For example, no phones after 6 PM or no internet after a certain time at night and so on. Follow your own rules – teach by example and be consistent. Children will pick up on your inconsistencies and later challenge you on them. When your children start secondary school, have open and honest discussions on the dangers of the internet, drugs and other issues. We spend much time indulging our children as we love them so much. But it is also important to teach discipline before it is too late. When your child enters teenage years, it is more difficult to suddenly introduce house rules and discipline as they are more likely to rebel. But if they grew up with certain house rules, then they are more accustomed to it. You may not want to use the term 'rules' if you feel that it's a negative word. You can be creative in how you teach discipline. Unfortunately, if there is no discipline, no boundaries, children grow up with a sense of entitlement and you would unknowingly do them a disfavour. As adults, they may face rejection, setbacks in life and they will struggle to process the new emotions, often leading to emotional dysregulation and relationship difficulties. It is also important to teach about the sustainability of the environment, recycling, the food sources, finances and even get them to work as volunteers so that they will appreciate the values of the society and learn work ethic. Parents assume that children get all their education from school, but this is not true. Parents have a responsibility to teach children about many social, environmental and issues. So, when your newly grown teenager throws a tantrum at you, don't mirror their behaviour by shouting back or lashing out. Show them how a responsible adult behaves. Remember, they are still learning from you and you are still responsible for their ultimate well-being. I have listed some quick reference points that you can apply if you are struggling with your teenage child, I have chosen to illustrate this more because I believe this is the age -group most parents struggle with. I have created this checklist using the principles of Rational Emotive Behaviour Therapy by Albert Ellis. Rational-emotive relationship therapy uses the cognitive behavioural approach to identify the emotional stressors, teaches to take responsibility for one's own emotional state. It offers choices not to be in the emotional state using emotional and behavioural techniques to achieve changes.

> Checking on your child's emotional well-being, every day with a simple greeting e.g., *Hi dear, how was your day? How are you?*

Acknowledging their emotional state and exploring further, for e.g., if they are angry or distressed you can say: *'I can see that you are upset'*. If you know the reason why they are upset you can acknowledge their cause of distress, offering them choices to help overcome the current emotional state. For e.g., *I understand that you are upset because (state the cause), I am here for you if you want to discuss your options on what to do next, I understand if you don't want to discuss this too as you want some space. I'll come back in a few minutes to check on you'*
Always keep the lines of communication open. Accept their emotional reaction as a type of communication and try to understand what message they are conveying. Pay attention to the non-verbal cues.
Avoiding direct criticism as much as possible, minimizing fault finding, and instead focusing on the strengths and positives.

Exercises

Write down a list of at least 5 qualities you appreciate in your spouse or partner and are grateful. E.g., the fact that your partner takes time every morning to drop the kids to school so that you have some extra time to yourself, etc.

Make a column next to each item that you are grateful for – how will you express your gratitude towards them.

Write down at least 1 -2 areas in your relationship, where you feel you can contribute more. E.g., spending more 1:1 quality time with each other, having a family meal over the weekend if you all lead busy lives.

How will you express your appreciation for your partner or friend in a creative way – to show how much you love them or care about them. E.g., baking a cake with their name on it.

Chapter 7 THE 4C APPROACH TO STRESS MANAGEMENT

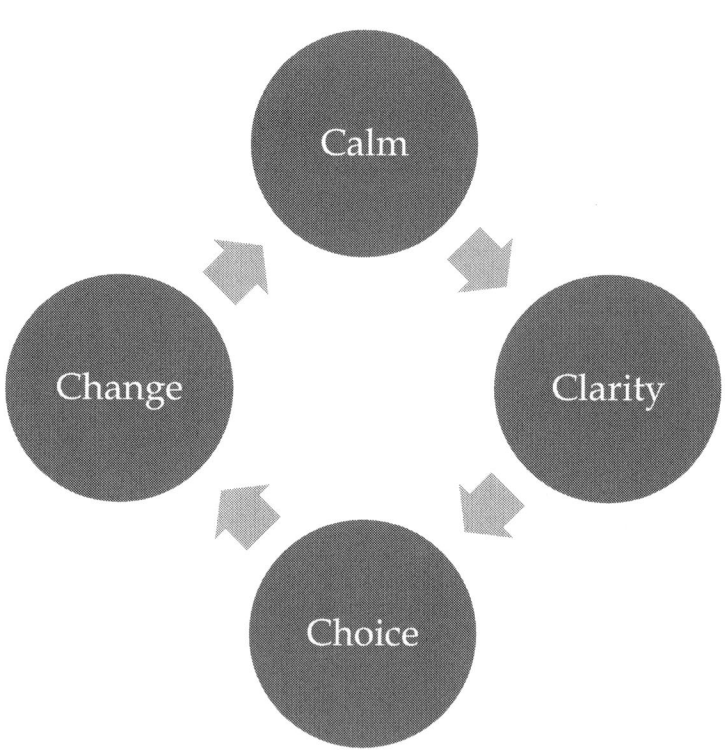

Step 1. CALM

DELAY   Analyze   Measured

As the name suggests, the first step is to avoid knee jerk responses to stressful situations. You can practise CALM as part of your daily habit so that you are well prepared to deal with day to day challenges of life. There are many tools to learn and practise CALM. I have listed the steps to CALM and will also share some tools to help you reach the state of CALM.

1. Delay the reaction to the stressful situation – for e.g., when tempted, do not send off that angry email!

2. Analyse the situation, think before you act, Step back and try to understand the complete picture – Pause for a few minutes.
3. Think before you communicate your feelings (esp. anger or resentment).
4. The goal here is to make a measured response.

Delay your reaction to a stressful situation with the help of some tools such as meditation, deep breathing, or mindfulness. When you are calm, your response will be different to when you are stressed and feeling overwhelmed. It is because stress usually triggers the fight or flight response – this is the drive for survival – driven by the primitive brain (limbic brain). But when we are calm, our rational brain (neocortex) makes the decisions and, our reaction will be driven by logical explanations, making informed decisions and a more thoughtful approach.

There are six basic emotions- anger, happiness, sadness, disgust, fear, and surprise. Whenever you face a stressful situation, analyse your emotional state – ask yourself – what emotion am I experiencing? As I have mentioned before, fear is one of the preceding primary emotions before stress. If you are experiencing fear, anger or sadness, it is helpful to understand and acknowledge the emotional state without attaching blame or guilt to it. Everyone experiences these emotions and it is natural to have emotions. Experience your emotional state with mindfulness, without trying to blame yourself or others for the emotions. Delay the need to act on your emotions. E.g., if you are experiencing anger, you do not have to act on this emotion immediately by having an anger outburst or an argument or sending off an email in anger. While you are entitled to experience different emotions, try to own the experience of the emotion as your own. You are responsible for the emotional state and you own it, when you take ownership of your emotions, you also take back the power (that you were earlier giving it away to others, by saying others are responsible for your emotional state). As you shift your emotional state to yourself and focus on yourself, you are feeling empowered. You then have choices that you can make. We will discuss Choice in step 3 in detail.

Tools that help you relax and be calm:

Meditation: The practice of meditation involves focussing the mind on a particular object, sound or thought – this is focussed meditation. There is another aspect of meditation where you let the mind wander and simply observe the mind going from one topic to the other without attaching any emotions to it. Some meditation techniques used are – Deep breathing exercises, body scan meditation, mantra meditation, affirmation meditation and so on. Mediation can be practised while lying down, standing up and even when walking. Yoga and tai chi are examples of meditation techniques that involve gentle exercise.

Exercise

Sit in a comfortable posture wearing light and comfortable clothes. Try to be in a quiet place and where you won't be disturbed for the next 15 minutes. As you sit, try to relax your muscles and close your eyes gently. Take deep breaths, as you inhale, mentally count to 4 and then exhale slowly to a count of 4 or more. Focus your mind on your breathing, notice the inhalation and exhalation. Repeat this slowly for the next 15minutes. You may notice your mind wandering off, having thoughts of events in the past or future events. Do not struggle with the mind, as soon as you realise that you mind has wandered off, gently bring it back to focus on your breathing. You can set a timer for 15 minutes if you wish. Some people listen to audio clips on meditation. This is called guided meditation. This may be helpful in the initial stages when you are starting to practise meditation.

Mindfulness: Mindfulness is the practice of being effortless, in a state free from any struggle, free from resistance – observing and experiencing the present moment, also known as 'here and now'. You can practice mindfulness at any moment of the day and does not need any preparation. You can practice it while eating, drinking, walking or working. You may have heard of the famous raisin exercise which most mindfulness therapists teach their clients. It involves appreciating, observing the raisin, using as many senses to examine, appreciate the source of the raisin, feel, taste and chew it slowly. You can apply the principles of mindfulness at work and at home. Mindfulness can be part of your meals where you prepare your plate, use the senses of your eyes and smell to appreciate and experience the aroma, the beautiful sight before you savour each bite. Mindfulness teaches us to slow down in our hectic lives and live in the moment. One can practise mindfulness with meditation and hence the two are inter-related.

Mood Diary: Keeping a mood diary needs some commitment, but it is worth the effort. You will feel more in control of your emotions as you will soon notice that you are recognising triggers for stress. This is also important if you have a history of depression and want to prevent a relapse or identify early signs of a recurrence. There are many ways to keep a log of your feelings and emotions:

Keep a mood journal where you write about your feelings in detail, and also write your thoughts, both negative and positive. You can write about things that have happened to you, reflecting on what cheered you up or upset you. You can jot down ideas about what helped you get through the day, whether it was watching a film or walking in the park. To help you get started, find a piece of paper or a notebook and start writing about today: how has it been so far? Has anything upset you or annoyed you? Write down what has cheered you up or lifted your mood (e.g., spending time with a loved one). Did you feel refreshed in the morning when you woke up? Did you have a good night's sleep? Has your mood fluctuated throughout the day? These are some of the questions you can think about. You can add as much detail as you want. For those who do not want to spend so much time, there are other options. You can download a mood diary app or use your pocket diary to jot down your emotional state. You can score your mood on a scale of 1–10 with 1 being the lowest mood and 10 being the best. You can even use smiley faces or icons as mood indicators.

Step 2. CLARITY

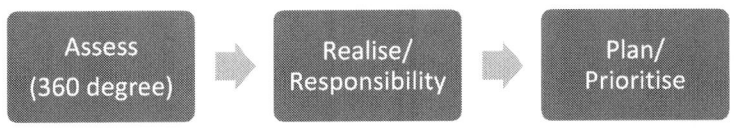

Exercise

Please see the following questions below, this is relevant to any unfulfilled project or struggle in your life:

- What are your goals?
- What is stopping you?
- What do you need to do to take action?
- Where do you want to be?

- What do you want to change?

You may want to revisit your wheel of life and get clarity.

The first step – CALM will help you achieve clarity over the situation. What is clarity in the context of stress? You will get the bigger picture instead of a snapshot image of the problem. For e.g., if you have been just given a speeding ticket, you are feeling anger and frustration over it, if you practice CALM, then you will see the bigger picture – i.e., speed cameras are there for a reason, the purpose is to improve safety on the roads, not just to penalise smart drivers. The reason you were speeding may be important to you but to the camera box, you were just another speeding driver. The bigger picture here is to save lives. When you get the bigger picture, you appreciate your role in the greater good of society. You bring out the altruistic part of you.

Clarity helps you focus on your bigger goals and not waste your energy over trivial matters. E.g., if you are feeling angry that a retailer just cheated you into buying a product that is not worth its value, you are naturally going to be angry. Imagine you bought this item to help you with your project work. Rather than dwelling on this issue for too long, you can plan your steps how to deal with this situation. Then divert your attention to your project – this is your focus and you soon realise that taking time away from your object of focus is ultimately going to cost you more money. Once you are clear of your focus, you will not spend too much time on situations that do not serve you constructively or positively.

Clarity helps you to be solution orientated rather than problem orientated. You think more clearly, how to resolve difficult or challenging situations.

Clarity can be achieved by information gathering and gives you a chance to reach out for more information, discuss with appropriate people what you are facing. Often when we are stressed, we tend to isolate ourselves and the problem is magnified. But when you are in the mode of seeking clarity, you have more opportunities to seek help, gain perspective and make well informed and rational decisions.

Tools that can help you achieve clarity are meditation, mindfulness, exercise, releasing your emotions (e.g., an outlet for your emotions through an activity such as boxing, breaking boards etc.)

Clarity also helps you plan your strategies on how to achieve solutions, realise your goals. Having a non-judgemental approach, information gathering and speaking to all parties concerned helps with clarity over the situation.

Exercise:

Take a balloon, (take deep breaths and blow the balloon slowly) this balloon metaphorically represents 'stress within you.' Blow this balloon as big as you want it to be – label it with a marker – you can name it after the person or situation you are currently experiencing stress from. E.g., work stress. Then try to feel its weight, play with it, imagine that the stress is out of your mind and it's all inside the balloon. Throw it gently on the air – see how it floats in the air, try to make friendship with the balloon, see it from a different perspective or angle. The stress is never a part of you, just like the balloon. The stress is external to you just like the balloon. You can decide what you want to do with the balloon – you could make it smaller, release some air or even burst it. The choice is yours. You are in charge of what you want to do with the balloon, which is now carrying your stress.

Step 3. CHOICE

After you have addressed steps 1 and 2, you are in a better position to think about your choices in any situation.

It is very difficult to consider the pros and cons of any situation when you are experiencing intense emotions – but when you are calm and have clarity over a stressful situation, you can then look at the choices available.

In this step you also analyse the situation, considering what the pros and cons of your action could be. If you acted in a certain way, what your gain or loss would be.

It is also helpful to consider any adverse event as an opportunity for learning and gaining experience.

Having the option to make choices in life can be empowering. Yet people are afraid to make bold choices in life such as changing jobs, changing career or ending a relationship. They prefer to be stuck in the situation because the fear of the unknown is far more daunting for them. Choices need not be perfect or risk proof. The fact that one can make choices in life in response to chronic stress can be a testimony that if you really want to get out of a situation, there is always a way.

Making choices is easier when it is a less significant decision such as changing a car after repeated breakdowns on the highway. But if you are stressed because of work, it is difficult to decide the best way out. Often people tend to blame themselves and shy away from seeking help, fearing that this will be held against them or be seen as a sign of weakness. Many people instead try to cope with stress by finding temporary escapes such as drinking alcohol or gambling which only makes the problem worse.

CIRCLE OF EXPERTISE: I want to introduce the circle of expertise here because, often when it comes to making important decisions about life, it is reassuring and uplifting to get a second opinion or a word of advice from our circle of friends and families. We often do not seek advice and miss out on practical and helpful advice from our loved ones. Everyone has their circle of expertise- this could be your ex-colleagues at work, college mentor or teacher, a friend who has a certain work experience, spouse, parents etc.

Exercise

Assessment exercise: Mr X is in his late 40s, he has a wife, 2 young children and is works as a banker and is the primary bread earner for his family. He received a letter from his boss to say that in the past month, Mr X arrived late to work on numerous occasions. Mr X had recently increased his intake of alcohol, often drinking excessively after work and has been experiencing morning hangovers. Mr X is much senior in age compared to his boss and had mentored his boss in the past. To get a formal warning from someone who was much younger to him in age and after serving in the bank was enough to hurt Mr X's pride.

By using steps 1, 2 and 3, how will you advise Mr X to react? Consider the choices Mr X has and what pros and cons could be of each step.

CHANGE

When you start implementing Calm, Clarity and Choice in your lives it is inevitable that you will see changes within you and surrounding you. If you had issues with your anger, you will notice changes in your temperament – you no longer are reacting on impulse.

Overtime, changes will become part of your habit, your unhelpful old habits that were hard wired to your brain will gradually fade away as you reprogram your brain forming new memories. Repeating a set of tasks over time becomes a habit and this in turn is hard wired to your brain as memory.

E.g., when you first started learning driving, you had to perform a series of hand and eye and leg coordinated movements, you repeated this over and over till they became hard wired to your brain and became memory. After some time, you notice that your eye, hand and legs automatically perform this new driving skill – almost like an autopilot. Similarly, when you practice a new set of skills over and over again soon it becomes a new habit.

Tools for CHANGE: I will discuss these tools further in chapter 8, titled 'Lifestyle Changes'.

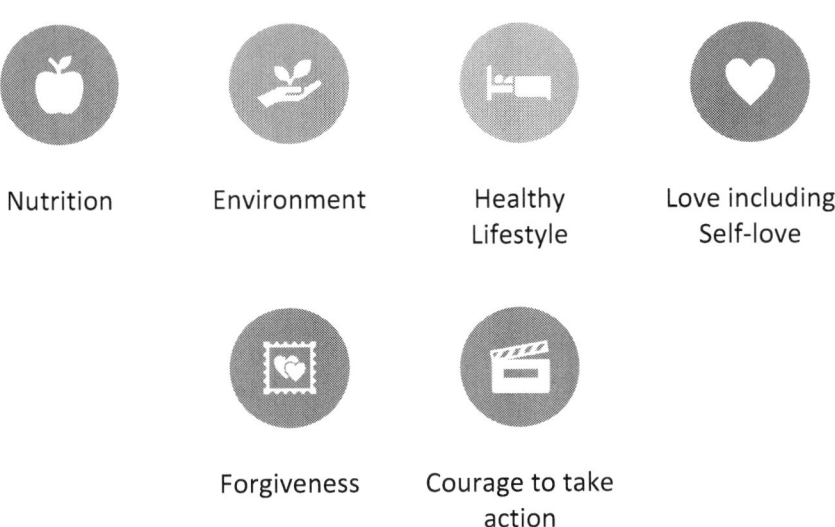

Nutrition   Environment   Healthy Lifestyle   Love including Self-love

Forgiveness   Courage to take action

Equipped with these new tools, you can set new goals for yourself and plan ahead. Set a time limit for realising your goals and make strategies to achieve your goals.

When you are more in control of your emotions, you can achieve more, as you will not be wasting energy and time procrastinating, ruminating or pitying yourself.

Chapter 8 MAKING LIFESTYLE CHANGES

Lifestyle is a combination of many factors such as sleep, nutrition, physical activity, social activities, health and wellbeing. I have focussed on some key lifestyle factors that are closely linked to Stress.

Nutrition: Paying attention to your diet is very important in managing stress, as I mentioned before that Stress can lead to physical health problems, poor diet and digestive issues can accelerate the onset of health problems. Heart burn, gastritis, indigestion and constipation are some of the commonest physical health problems that are associated with poor diet. Eating too little, skipping meals or eating a lot of junk food at once can lead to health problems.

Some of the items to avoid in excess are sugar, caffeine, and alcohol. Each one is related to a host of chronic health conditions as follows:

- Diabetes
- Heart disease
- Raised Cholesterol
- Fatty Liver, Cirrhosis and Liver failure linked to alcohol dependency,

Cut down on smoking to limit the intake of nicotine. Smoking has been linked to lung cancer and other chronic lung conditions. Unfortunately, people rely on nicotine, alcohol and other addictive substances to cope with stress, ignoring the fact that these are in itself potential for triggering health problems which aggravates stress in the long run. These are quick fixes which do not work in the long term.

Environment: Take care of your environment, making sure your home and workspace has:

- Adequate light
- Fresh air

- Comfortable desk space, comfortable chair supporting good posture
- No loud noise

Exercise - Exercise or physical activity has many other benefits: it helps with weight reduction, reduces the risk of heart disease, and helps to regulate blood sugar. Exercise also improves sleep and strengthens bones and muscles, thus improving the overall quality of life. While considering which form of exercise best suits your needs, it is helpful to have a physical check-up. Generally, a mild form of exercise, such as walking is suitable for people with most health conditions. Once you have identified your preferred type of activity, try to exercise at least twice weekly for the best results. According to NHS recommendations, it's essential to do a combination of aerobic exercise (such as walking, running, badminton) and strength exercise (such as weight lifting, push-ups). Stretching the muscles is also essential. Example of different types of activities:

Yoga: Yoga is unique because it is both a form of exercise and meditation. Controlled breathing, postures, and strengthening moves form essential components of yoga. Yoga originated more than 5,000 years ago in India and has been mentioned in ancient Indian scriptures known as the Vedas. In the last few decades, yoga has gained immense popularity in the West, with yoga centers springing up in major cities. One of the reasons it is so popular is its simplicity and the enormous health benefits associated with it.

Activities you can do to relax, and this will also divert your attention from the ruminative thoughts and stress:

Going for a walk in the park, walking your dog

and any other light physical activity
Colouring, mindful colouring, painting and any other artwork
Watching a movie, or your favourite TV show
Volunteering at your local charity and socialising
Listening to music
Cooking or Baking

Chapter 9 Self-compassion, Self-love & positive affirmations

Failures can be opportunities to learn. We get sucked in the 'here and now,' and miss the opportunities that come with any setback. The founder of Microsoft, Bill Gates, was a college dropout, but he went on to build Microsoft, that made him the richest man. It is ok to fail, no matter what the society labels you. Your life will change when you stop focusing on what others think of you and focus on what makes you fulfilled and content.

Exercise:

Ask yourself the following questions:

- What activity makes me happy and time stands still when I'm doing it?
- What do I want to do with the rest of my life?

- Do I see myself happy and fulfilled in this job for the next 10 or 20 years, do I believe that circumstances will change for the better?
- How do I arrange the following in order of my priorities – money, security, comfort, health, relationships, education, children, property or assets, business, job or career, hobbies and so on? You can add more categories to your list.
- If I'm struggling in area of my life, do I believe that I can improve things for the better? Do I have a plan to make things better?

When we have setbacks or failure in our lives, it teaches us many lessons that we can apply in the future. If we keep an open mind to adversity, we will learn more about our preferences and our choices. For example, when you have a situation where you invested say some money to buy a software or a product and you soon found out that the product is not suitable for you, you can then plan future purchases where you can avoid the software in all your applications and so on. It is never too late to move on from a mistake – it is only a problem if you feel that you need to stick to it because it's now too late to move on, a concept known as learned helplessness – it is relevant in case of relationships too.

Love your own company: Have a 'me' time to nurture yourself, pamper yourself, go for a movie, have a spa day or simply read a book. There are many ways you can have quality time with yourself. Sometimes people start to panic at the thought of being left alone or being outcast from a group. But every situation can be interpreted in a positive way. Silence is sometimes a great teacher, when you spend a quiet time with yourself and your mind is in a state of calm and quiet, you can practice meditation which brings with it, mental peace and inspiration to act.

Many great motivators practice regular meditation and have quiet time on their own – they practice self-love and self-compassion.

Oprah Winfrey, the TV personality and a great advocate of empowerment, has portrayed the message of empowerment through practising self-love, self-forgiveness and self-compassion.

I understand that it may be difficult to love yourself if you are fighting with self-guilt over the past and feeling depressed. Depression is closely associated with feelings of guilt. Stress can lead to depression. That is why it is vital to practice self-love the same way as one would go to the gym to improve physical fitness.

Practising regular mental exercises is as important as practising physical exercises. You do not need to wait for a stressful event to start practising meditation or going through affirmations every day. This can be part of your daily routine just as you have routine for going to work or washing the clothes, as an example.

Positive affirmations help to refocus on goals when someone is experiencing negative thoughts or self-doubt.

This is a way of practicing self-love, self-appreciation, and self-acceptance.

I have written a script as an example of an affirmation dialogue below. You could record this on your phone and listen to it several times a day.

I want to focus on my breathing today, I generally do not pay attention to my breathing but for the next few minutes today, I will breathe consciously. I want to experience the sensation of breathing in and out. As I inhale, I can feel the air touching my nose, passing through my windpipe and filling my lungs. My lungs are experiencing deep appreciation for Mother Nature who is providing this clean air. I am aware that the oxygen is being used up by my cells to nourish the body. I am taking in nourishment and I am giving out waste from my body. I next want to nourish my mind. I want to breathe in positivity and breathe out negativity. Today I want to declutter my mind and brain, over the years my brain has accumulated many unwanted memories of people I no longer meet or will be meeting. My mind has many anxieties of the future that seem improbable to occur. I waste valuable time and energy each day arranging and going through this wardrobe of memories and negative thoughts in my mind and brain that deplete my energy and productivity. I want to get rid of this junkyard. Today I will call in the skippers and declutter my mind and brain so that I can feel renewed, energised and breathe in new life. My talents, my genius is being overshadowed by other people's views and opinions. I have lived my life conforming to what others want from me. I have prioritised other's wishes over mine. Life is precious, I cannot get back the years that I have lost, but

I want to live the future feeling positive and full of positivity. Only I can make the changes, I must stop expecting my circumstances to change or the people to change in order to feel positive. I must stop giving away the keys to my peace, happiness and prosperity to others. I must take back control and I must be in charge. This is no longer just a passing thought. It is now my fullest desire and aspiration to live the life of my dreams. It is time for my dreams to manifest, time for a new beginning and time for me to take action. I must stop the cycle of repeated hurt, blame and self-pity. I must rise up and dust off the negativity that is still holding tight on me. I must replace fear with courage, replace doubts with belief in me. I (say your name) am in charge of my destiny, I (repeat your name) will take action to make my dreams become reality.

Continue to take in deep breaths in and out for next few minutes and slowly open your eyes.

Chapter 10 Conclusion

I hope I have raised some awareness on the impact of Stress on our lives and why it is so important to look after our emotional well-being. I hope that employers recognise the importance of maintaining a stress-free working environment. If you are an employer or a business owner, please take steps to boost the morale of your staff by addressing Stress at work. Don't assume that the problems will go away by itself.

At home, it is important to maintain good work-life balance. Resist the temptation to bring work to your home unless you work from home. Give time and space to your loved ones. When you give away your precious time and energy towards building a better relationship, you will also gain many folds.

Thrive for higher goals, bigger and better future, when you dream big, you will automatically find courage, strength and inspiration to deal with stressful situations in a more positive way.

To be the ideal leader, you must lead by example, be empathic, a good listener and an optimist. Good leadership skills are integral to the success of any business or corporate organisation. You are not a born leader, but you can learn to be a good leader. Find out your leadership style, there are few ways to find this out – personality assessments such as the Myers Briggs personality assessment is a useful tool.

To stand out in adversity needs courage and resilience, everyone has the ability to be successful in life and to be happy in what they do.

REFERENCES:

Aguilera, Greti (1 January 2011). "HPA axis responsiveness to stress: Implications for healthy aging". Experimental Gerontology. 46 (2–3): 90–95.

AXA Stress Index 2017. A survey conducted by One Poll on 4000 UK adults. https://www.axa.co.uk/contentassets/8e9f9aa1be a143b8b30b8495292b241a/axa-stress-index-2017.pdf/

Black C (2008) Dame Carol Black's Review of the Health of Britain's Working Age Population: Working for a healthier tomorrow. London: TSO.

Brown GW, Harris T. Social origins of depression: a reply. Psychol Med. 1978;8:577–88

Ellis A., Dryden W. (1997). The Practice of Rational-Emotive Behavior Therapy. New York, NY: Springer Publishing Company. [Google Scholar]

Health Executive Agency (2017) Work-related stress, depression or anxiety statistics in Great Britain 2017.

Hammer MS, et al. "Environmental Noise Pollution in the United States: Developing an Effective Public Health Response." Environ Health Perspect. 2014;122(2),115-119.

Jackson, Mark (2014), Cantor, David; Ramsden, Edmund (eds.), "Evaluating the Role of Hans Selye in the Modern History of Stress", Stress, Shock, and Adaptation in the Twentieth Century, Open Access Monographs and Book Chapters Funded by Wellcome Trust, University of Rochester Press, ISBN 9781580464765,

Jorn, A. (2018). Rational Emotive Behavior Therapy. Psych Central. Retrieved on August 25, 2019, from https://psychcentral.com/lib/rational-emotive-behavior-therapy/

Khansari D.; Murgo A.; Faith R. (May 1990). "Effects of stress on the immune system". Immunology Today. 11 (5): 170–175.

Klengel T, Pape J, Binder EB, et al. The role of DNA methylation in stress-related psychiatric disorders. Neuropharmacology. 2014;80:115–32.

Koops, Matthias (2010), "Historical Account of the Substances Which have been Used to Describe Events, and to Convey Ideas, from the Earliest Date, to the Invention of Paper", Cambridge University Press, pp. 7–258, ISBN 9780511694530

Lancet, T. (2017). Improving mental health in the workplace. The Lancet, 390(10107), 2015.

Lazarus RS, Cohen JB. "Environmental Stress. Human Behavior and Environment." In: Altman I, et al, eds. Human Behavior and Environment. New York, NY: Plenum Press; 1977:89-127.

MacLean, P.D. (1952). "Some psychiatric implications of physiological studies on frontotemporal portion of limbic system (visceral brain)". Electroencephalography and Clinical Neurophysiology. 4 (4): 407–418.

Mental Health Foundation (May 2018). Stress: Are we coping? London Mental Health Foundation

Mind and Body Approaches for Stress: What the Science Says." National Center for Complementary and Integrative Health. U.S. Department of Health & Human Services. Jan. 2016

Myers, Isabel Briggs with Peter B. Myers (1995) [1980]. Gifts Differing: Understanding Personality Type. Mountain View, CA: Davies-Black Publishing. ISBN 978-0-89106-074-1

Radley JJ, Kabbaj M, Jacobson L, Heydendael W, Yehuda R, Herman JP. Stress risk factors and stress-related pathology: neuroplasticity, epigenetics and endophenotypes. Stress. 2011;14(5):481-497.

Reichmann F, Holzer P. Neuropeptide Y: A stressful review. Neuropeptides. 2016;55:99-109. doi:10.1016/j.npep.2015.09.008

Rothmann S, Coetzer EP (24 October 2003). "The big five personality dimensions and job performance". SA Journal of Industrial Psychology. 29.

Schneiderman, Neil; Ironson, Gail; Siegel, Scott D. (1 January 2005). "STRESS AND HEALTH: Psychological, Behavioral, and Biological Determinants". Annual Review of Clinical Psychology. 1: 607-628.

Selye, Hans (1 January 1950). "The physiology and pathology of exposure to stress". APA PsycNET.

Spruill, Tanya M. (7 February 2017). "Chronic Psychosocial Stress and Hypertension". Current

Hypertension Reports. 12 (1): 10–16. Stephens, Mary Ann C.; Wand, Gary (1 January 2012). "Stress and the HPA Axis". Alcohol Research : Current Reviews. 34 (4): 468–483.

Ulrich-Lai, Yvonne M.; Herman, James P. (7 February 2017). "Neural Regulation of Endocrine and Autonomic Stress Responses". Nature Reviews Neuroscience. 10 (6): 397–409.

Widmaier, Eric P. (2015). Vander's Human Physiology: The Mechanisms Of Body Function. Boston: McGraw-Hill Education. p. 182. ISBN 978-1-259-60779-0.

World Health Organisation . International Statistical Classification of Diseases and Related Health Problems: ICD-10.Geneva: Switzerland: World Health Organisation; 1992.

FURTHER READING:

https://www.gov.uk/government/publications/the-nhs-constitution-for-england

https://www.nice.org.uk/guidance/ng13

https://www.nice.org.uk/guidance/qs147

Myers-Briggs Type Indicator (MBTI)

http://www.hse.gov.uk/pubns/indg424.pdf

ABOUT THE AUTHOR:

Dr Sarmila Sinha is a Consultant Psychiatrist, Author and Motivational Speaker based in the UK. She is a member of the Royal College of Psychiatrists and Fellow of the Complementary Medical Association. Dr Sinha has been a Health and Well-Being Ambassador for doctors in the NHS and has over 15 years of experience as a Psychiatrist in the UK. She is the founder of Living Life Stress Free Ltd, a registered college of the Complementary Medical Association, providing Stress Management courses and workshops to professionals and entrepreneurs.

Dr Sinha has a passion for raising awareness on mental health issues among the general public and reducing stigma in mental health. Her book *'Depression A Guide to Recovery',* is an uplifting and actionable guide to the causes, symptoms, treatment and management of Depression. *'My goal was to create a resource that gets right to the point, and reaches out to people in despair, in a way that's comforting,' she* explains.

Dr Sinha believes in a holistic approach to treatment and emphasises the importance of reducing stress and managing stress to prevent chronic physical and mental illnesses. She respects traditional practices – Eastern Health practice such as Yoga, Meditation and Tai Chi, to name a few, which can be effectively used to manage Stress.

Her inspiration to become an author and motivational speaker comes from her passion and efforts to raise awareness on health topics such as well-being, stress management, work-life balance, improving relationships, conflict resolution, improving resilience and leadership skills.

Her motto is 'Everyone has the potential to be a genius. Be positive and Believe in yourself. If you can Dream, you can Live It too.'

Notes:

An Expert Guide to Stress Management

Printed by Amazon Italia Logistica S.r.l.
Torrazza Piemonte (TO), Italy